Fragments

Shalini Singh

BookLeaf Publishing

India | USA | UK

Made with ❤ on the BookLeaf Publishing Platform
www.bookleafpub.in
www.bookleafpub.com

Dedication

To all the souls who've felt deeply,

who've broken, healed,and kept writing

anyway --

this book is for you.

Preface

This book is a collection of moments—some whispered, some wept, and some wondered aloud.
Each poem came to me like a quiet visitor, carrying fragments of memory, emotion, and reflection.
Writing them was not just an act of expression, but of healing.

You may find yourself in a few lines, or lose yourself in others.
Either way, I hope these words sit beside you like an old friend—softly, sincerely, without judgment.

Thank you for turning these pages.
Thank you for listening.
Shalini Singh

Acknowledgements

Thank you to those who encouraged me to write,
who listened, supported, or simply believed in me.
Also thank you to those who didn't believe in me,
because pain often gives birth to poetry
Your presence made this book possible.

1. Words

Words

What are words?
Who formed words?
Why do we need words?
Who first used words?

All these questions are just subjects of Etymology.

The feelings we have,
The emotion of pain & love finds meaning through
words.
But what about the emotion that lies somewhere
between pain & pleasure:
Between love & hate:
Between joy & sadness?
Do we have words for that also?

All these words,
Whatever the language be:
Can they truly express our emotions?
Can they describe our feelings in entirety?

These tiny little bits of feelings,

That possess us sometimes:
Like a tiny, naughty cloud
Quickly vanishing from the sky - there it was ,there
gone.

Do any words justify these emotions?
Of pain & pleasure; love & hate; joy & sadness?

2. Mother

Mother

Every mother is a warrior.
One who protects her child,
One who stands for the child.

Some mothers may not be strong to fight always,
But
Mothers they are nonetheless.
Being there for their child, feeling for them.

A child grows up to be a
Man or a woman -
But
A mother always will be a mother.

That's the cycle of life!

3. Someone

Someone

Wish someone special, to talk to me.
Whisper love to me, know me, my thoughts & my
dreams.

Someone to cherish me,
Be with me, enjoy me.
Give those featherly kisses to me.
Touch me occasionally, knowingly.
A peck here & a pat there.
Someone who hugs me,
Who loves me enough to share themselves
And their life in entirety.

4. Map of Scars

There is a map—
A map etched not on paper,
But across my being.
A Map of Scars.

Some scars are physical—
Born of accidents, cuts, and burns.
They've faded with time,
Tucked away beneath the skin.

But deeper still are the emotional wounds—
The ones no one sees,
Yet shape the way I breathe, react, exist.

They show up as irritation,
As restlessness,
As anger that flares without warning.

When I was betrayed, again and again,
A deep Welt formed—
One that still aches in silence.

When I was ignored, left alone in the noise,
A bright, Burning spot appeared,

One that still sometimes singes.

When I was spoken down to,
Dismissed and diminished,
A Blister swelled—raw and tender,
One that oft pains me still.

The physical scars have long since healed,
But the emotional ones...
They linger.
They map my pain, my survival—
And they may remain
For ages yet to come.

5. Faith

Everything is falling apart!
What a devastation it is.
Living on the edge of emotions,
It now feels like the cup is empty.

But no,
there is still something to live for,
something that'll never die.
The Love will always be there,
And faith{God} will never end.

Life is faith, strength and hope.
It's an on & on struggle to live,
To move forward.

What if there are so many obstacles on the way,
I have to live & move ahead.

You{God} are with me,
And that is all that matters.
Now I will never lose hope.

6. Rain

I was standing in the middle of the road.
Suddenly it started raining.

I have always loved being in the rain.
The soft pitter-patter of the raindrops;
As tiny diamonds they come to meet the Earth.
The soft aroma of wet mud is so exotic .

When I was young
I used to play in the rain,
Jumping in the puddles;
Making paper boats & playing;
Coming home all drenched'

Now also, I am enjoying the rain.
Standing in the middle of the road.

I am so happy the rains have come .
It's so easy now to hide my tears.

7. If My Walls Could Talk

If my walls could talk,
What secrets would they spill?
Would they sing of love and joy,
Of gentle mornings bathed in light,
Of whispers wrapped in tenderness,
Of laughter filling every crack,
Of hands held in quiet resolve,
Of dreams nurtured by hopeful hearts?

Or would they murmur in the dark,
Of tears soaked into silent corners,
Of cold words etched in plaster,
Of tension thick as shadows at dusk,
Of blame ricocheting off the paint,
Of bruised memories clinging to the brick,
Of voices lost in endless battles?

If my walls could talk,
Would they speak of growth,
Of learning to forgive and heal?
Or would they recall the weight of regret,
The silence after storms,
The ache of words unsaid?

Perhaps they'd do both—
Tell of love's fragile bloom,
And of wounds that never fade,
Revealing truths in half-light,
Neither all joy nor all pain,
But stories woven of both—
Only, if my walls could talk.

8. Echo of Kindness

Those beautiful eyes,
That had witnessed the world for eighty-two years,
Would live on, even in death—
Her father had said so, softly, surely.

A gift, they called it—
One met with praise and quiet awe.
But no one spoke
Of how kindness echoes in ways unseen.

Five years passed.
Now her mother, frail and fading,
Needed new eyes—
And she was given them.

What strange hand writes such stories?
Was it fate, weaving lines in silence?
Or just a poetic coincidence?

She wonders still—
Or was it the echo
Of a kindness once given,
Now returned?

9. Her Morning Rule

It's 7 a.m., the morning's hush—
She rises slowly from her bed.
Alone again, yet not undone,
These quiet hours are hers to thread.

No footsteps echo down the hall,
No voices call her name aloud.
But solitude becomes her throne,
A queen beneath the waking cloud.

What she needs now is simple, clear—
A moment still, a sacred pause.
A cup of coffee, dark and strong,
No sugar, cream, or needless gloss.

This bitter brew, her ritual fire,
Her secret strength, her silent muse.
It stirs her blood, ignites desire,
A power she alone can use.

In every sip, a bold restart,
A rhythm beating in her chest.
She faces day with open heart—
Alone, yes—but fully equipped.

10. At the Corner of My Eyes

There's a window on the side of my room—
A little frame to glimpse the world through.

A small kitty darts past,
Purring softly, chasing shadows with grace.

A boy on a bicycle speeds by,
Newspapers tucked under his arm,
The rustle of headlines in his wake.

A cop stands near the corner,
Stroking his moustache,
A quiet smile playing on his lips—lost in thought,
perhaps.

The shopkeeper gestures animatedly,
Hands flying in the air,
Bargaining with customers,
Woven into the hum of the street.

And then—
A couple walks by,
Hand in hand,

Wrapped in each other,
As if the world had paused just for them.

All this,
At the corner of my eyes,
Through a window
That quietly watches life unfold.

11. The River's Reflection

Have you ever wondered
How life mirrors a river?

When the river is born in the mountains,
It gushes forth—clear, wild, untamed.
Its waters are pure, fearless, full of song—
Just like a newborn,
Trusting, vibrant, untouched by the world.

As it flows into the plains,
It slows—just a little.
Still full of energy,
But now aware of its path.
Like a teenager—
Reckless, yet learning caution.

Further down, the river begins to carry weight.
Silt, debris, the traces of every place it's touched.
It winds more deliberately now—
Mature, grounded, but still restless.
Like youth—
Thoughtful, strong, and sometimes stubborn.

And then—

It approaches the ocean.
Its current tired, its voice softer.
No longer rushing—just flowing.
As if surrendering to something greater.
Like an old man,
Worn by time, unsure, but ready.

The river meets its end,
Or perhaps—its beginning.
Just as life does.

12. Empty Nest

There was a time—
When this house pulsed with life.
Laughter bouncing off the walls,
Endless chatter,
Silly arguments over nothing and everything.

Birthdays were grand.
Friends pouring in,
Wrapping paper flying,
Gifts opened long past bedtime.

Mornings?
A mad rush.
No time for me, no time for breath.
But somehow—everything got done.
Late, messy, chaotic—but done.

There were school projects—
Due tomorrow, started tonight.
Craft paper, glue sticks, a late-night run to the store.

Exams.
Stress.
Coffee in hand.

Tired eyes and tight hugs.
Then came results—
The joy, the tears, the jumping in the hallway.
We made it through. Together.

Outside, birds chirped like they were part of the chaos.
Even the squirrels danced.
Even the walls listened.

Now—
It's quiet.

So quiet
It hums in my ears.
Sometimes the phone rings,
And it's them.
Sometimes.

The nest is empty now...
But the heart?
The heart is overflowing—
With echoes of little feet,
Late-night talks,
Bedtime stories and slammed doors.

Memories.
Every one a jewel.

Brighter than gold.
Carved deep into the soul of this home.

13. The Night

It was a new moon night,
Darkness spread its silent wings,
A heavy blanket over the Earth.
Thunder roared, winds howled,
Lightning slashed the sky,
Briefly tearing the veil of night.

But deeper still was the storm within her—
A tempest raging through every vein.
It was the darkest night of her soul,
Where even hope had turned to ash.

That night, she thought of leaving,
Of slipping away into silence.
But then—she remembered her child.
His face, his laugh, his need for her.
And for him, she chose to stay.

Then came the miracle—
A quiet dawn unlike any before.
The night, once merciless and endless,
Melted into the most radiant sunrise.
And in that light,

She found herself again.

14. Loneliness and Solitude

What's the difference between solitude and loneliness?
Loneliness—I've known all my life.
It was my silent companion since childhood,
With few friends to play with,
Even fewer voices to confide in.

I grew up wrapped in that quiet ache.
When I married, I thought—
At last, a partner to walk beside me.
I believed my loneliness would fade.

But little did I know—
Marriage can deepen the silence.
Sometimes, it makes you feel even more alone.
And so I drifted,
More isolated than ever before.

Time passed.
I fought it. I fumed.
But the emptiness stayed.

Then, something shifted—
Not outside, but within.
I stopped resisting.

I surrendered to the stillness.

And slowly,
My loneliness transformed.
It no longer haunted me—
It held me gently.

Now, I call it solitude.
And strangely,
I've come to enjoy its company.

15. Bibliosmia

In the precious halls of old libraries deep,
I'm intoxicated by the scent of books that sleep,
A world of words, where stories whisper low,
Of forgotten places, where tales unfold and grow.

Since childhood, books have been my guiding light,
A realm of wonder, where imagination takes flight,
Glorious histories, disturbing truths revealed,
Courageous heroes, cowardly hearts that concealed.

In pages worn, new worlds are born anew,
Fabulous realms, dystopian futures in view,
Paper and ink, a portal to explore,
A universe of thoughts, where wisdom is stored.

The smell of old books, a bibliophile's delight,
Transports me to realms both enchanting and bright,
A sensory journey, where the past comes alive,
In the musty scent, a world of stories thrives.

16. The Himalayas

For centuries, they have stood—
Tall, mighty, and unmoved.
Towering above the world,
The majestic Himalayas—
Crowned with immaculate clouds,
Playing hide and seek with the sun.

Robed in snow, pure as milk,
They guard uncharted caves,
Veil treacherous paths,
And host the fury of fierce avalanches.
Glaciers carve through their spine,
Ancient and ever-flowing.

They've watched travelers come and go—
Pilgrims, wanderers, seekers of truth.
They are the sacred abode of Shiva,
Whose breath dances in the mountain air.
The hallowed Ganga is born from their heart,
A river kissed by the divine.

Mystics and sages dwell in their shadows,
Monks vanish into the mist,
Carrying questions only silence can answer.

The Himalayas—
Timeless witnesses to kingdoms that rose and fell,
Empires now dust upon the wind.
Here, the wind sings songs
Only eagles understand.

Footsteps may fade,
But stories echo through stone.
Even silence kneels
At the feet of these ancient giants.

Where the soul remembers what the world forgets.

अस्त्युत्तरस्यां दिशि देवतात्मा हिमालयो नाम नगाधिराजः।

17. Awakening

Awake she is now—
After a decade of silence and sleep.
No, she is no sleeping beauty,
But an ordinary woman,
Who has lived an extraordinary storm.

From the slumber of pain she rises—
Years weighed with disrespect,
Centuries carved by quiet endurance,
Eons of being shaped, used, and silenced.

But something shifted.
In the stillness,
She began to listen to her own breath.
To cradle her wounds
And call them sacred.

It is a new dawn for her now.
She no longer seeks mirrors to reflect her worth.
She has found her own light—
Soft, steady, and sovereign.

She smiles at her reflection,
Not for how she looks,

But for the fire she survived.

The treasure she longed for
Was never out there.
She found it buried deep within—
The quiet hum of the Universe
Beating in her chest.

She has awakened the power of Durga,
And dances now with the rage of Kali—
Not to destroy, but to protect
The temple she has become.

She is not the same.
She is more.
Whole.
Holy.
Home.

18. The River in My Veins

I have been a work in progress—
Not just for years,
But for centuries.
What I am today
Is carved from ages of hardship and toil.

The blood in my veins
Carries the stories of those
Who lived, struggled, and survived—
Ancestors long gone,
Yet pulsing through me still.

Their trauma, though unspoken,
Shaped the contours of my psyche.
My blood remembers—
Their lullabies and their screams.

It whispers tales of heartbreak and harvest,
Of hymns sung by firelight,
Of losses borne and legacies sown.

I walk with their shadows,
Under the same moon that once lit their paths.

The mountains they braved
Call out to me for courage.
The rivers and trees echo traditions
Passed quietly through time.

Not all inheritance is seen—
But it shapes my breath,
My choices,
My silence.

Ancestry flows like water
Through bloodlines unseen.
And I—
I am the river's newest curve,
Shaped gently,
Powerfully,
By all who came before me.

19. The Music of Silence

Silence hums a gentle tune—
hear the birds chirp,
the bees softly hum,
the air whisper through branches,
leaves rustling like quiet applause.

There is music in stillness.

Silence heals.
In the hush of a forest,
by a still lake at dawn,
nature invites us
to be truly alive—
without a single word.

It cradles our wounds,
gives emotions space to breathe.
Tears fall freely,
and in their quiet flow,
cleansing happens—
healing begins.

Silence speaks the language of the divine,
where the soul listens

to what the ears cannot hear.

In its stillness, the ego dissolves.
What remains is presence.
And in presence—God.

20. The Paradox of Desire

When I was young, all I wanted was to grow up—
to be free, independent, in charge of my life.
Now that I'm grown, I miss the simplicity of childhood—
the laughter, the lightness, the absence of responsibility.

Back then, I thought money would solve everything.
Now I have enough,
but I often long for those days
when happiness came without a price tag.

I used to dream of love like in fairy tales—
Prince Charming and all.
And now that I have a home, a partner, a family,
I find myself missing the quiet comfort of my father's
care.

It's strange, isn't it?
How we chase things thinking they'll make us whole,
only to realize
that every desire fulfilled births another.

The more we get,
the more we seem to want.
And so, the circle continues—

never fully satisfied.

But maybe the answer was never outside.
Maybe real fulfillment comes from within.
Because once you find peace inside yourself,
desire doesn't disappear...
it just stops being loud.

21. Hues of Love

The bee adored the bloom—
its nectar, sweet intoxication.
Drawn by delight,
it danced on velvet petals,
forgetting time,
forgetting everything
but the ecstasy of now.
But as the sun dipped low,
the petals gently closed.
And by dawn,
the bee lay still—
a silent victim
of love's fleeting embrace.

Elsewhere, the candle burned bright,
its flame proud and unwavering.
The fly, entranced by its golden glow,
whirled ever closer—
lost in the trance
of luminous affection.
The candle, in its passion,
gave everything—
melting, weeping,
just to keep the fly warm.

It died a quiet death,
wrapped in the wings of longing.

The sky loves the Earth deeply—
sending rain as kisses,
and thunder as cries.
Yet they never touch,
held apart by distance,
joined only through
storms and sunsets.

Each night, the tide rises—
pulled by the moon's silent longing.
The moon never descends.
The tide never questions.
Still, they dance—
lovers bound
by a yearning
they'll never fulfill.

Love is ecstatic.
Love is divine.
But love can also consume.

It gives.
It glows.
It forgets itself

in the fire it sets.

For in true love—
one blooms,
one burns,
and both
are never the same again.

Yet—

From the ashes,
a fragrance lingers.
From the waves,
a rhythm is born.
From the ache,
a softer heart takes shape.

And though love may leave us changed,
what it leaves behind—
is grace.
A quiet knowing,
that even in longing,
we lived.